The Gigantic Book of Bible Puzzles

Standard PUBLISHING

Cincinnati, Ohio

The Gigantic Book of Bible Puzzles

Published by Standard Publishing, Cincinnati, Ohio
www.standardpub.com

Compilation Copyright © 2011 by Standard Publishing

All rights reserved. Permission is granted to reproduce these pages for classroom purposes only—not for resale.

#35385. Manufactured in Newburyport, MA, USA, March 2012.

Project Editor: Marcy Levering
Art direction and cover design: Sandy Wimmer

All Scripture quotations, unless otherwise indicated, are taken from the *HOLY BIBLE, NEW INTERNATIONAL VERSION®. NIV®.* Copyright © 1973, 1978, 1984, 2011 by Biblica, Inc.™ Used by permission of Zondervan. All rights reserved.

ISBN: 978-0-7847-3183-3

17 16 15 14 13 12   3 4 5 6 7 8 9 10 11

Everything from Nothing

Only God can create something from nothing. When he [made] our world and the whole universe around us, he simply spoke words [and] things came into being. To find out what God named the things he made, [follow] each path from God's words to the thing he made. If you need [help, you] can read Genesis 1.

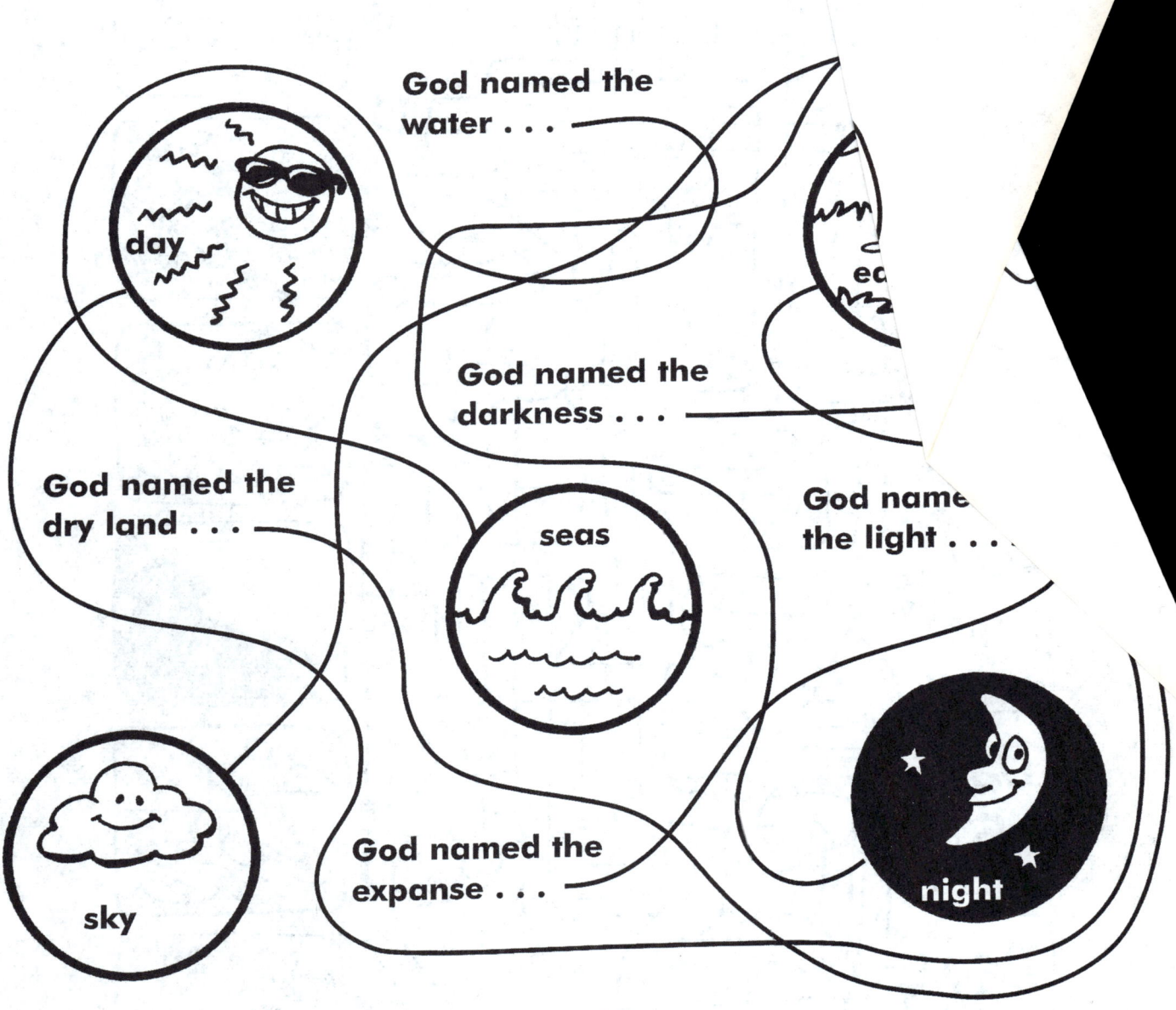

Genesis 1

Let There Be . . .

Starting with ..., find the correct path through the maze to the things that Go... on that day. Do this until you have matched all the days with ... pictures. Read Genesis 1:1-25 if you need help.

Genesis 1

Creative Counting

See how much you know about the days of creation. Use the words in the tree to complete the puzzle. You can check your answers in Genesis 1.

ACROSS

1. On which day did God create man and woman?
4. On which day did God create fish and fowl?
5. What did God do on the seventh day?
7. On which day did God create the sun and moon?

DOWN

2. On which day did God create trees and grass?
3. On which day did God create day and night?
6. On which day did God create the sky?

Genesis 1

So Many Animals

God made the animals of the sea and sky and earth. To find out what God thought of all he had done, write the first letter of each animal in the box next to it. Read in Genesis 1 how God created everything.

looked at everything he had made, and it was very